FRANK THOMAS
POWER HITTER

BY BILL GUTMAN

MILLBROOK SPORTS WORLD
THE MILLBROOK PRESS
BROOKFIELD, CONNECTICUT

Photographs courtesy of Allsport: cover, pp. 3, 34, 43 (all by Jonathan Daniel), 44 (Otto Gruele), 46 (Jonathan Daniel); Focus on Sports: cover inset, pp. 22, 27, 31; AP/Wide World Photos: pp. 4, 24-25, 28-29, 33, 36-37, 38, 39, 40; Elite Photography: p. 9; Larry Cutchall/*Columbus Ledger-Enquirer*: p. 10; Auburn University: pp. 13, 16, 19.

Library of Congress Cataloging-in-Publication Data
Gutman, Bill.
Frank Thomas: power hitter / by Bill Gutman.
p. cm.— (Millbrook sports world)
Includes index.
Summary: A biography of the power-hitting baseball player, from his childhood in Georgia through his college days at Auburn University to his professional career with the Chicago White Sox.
ISBN 1-56294-569-6
1. Thomas, Frank, 1968- —Juvenile literature. 2. Baseball players—United States—Biography—Juvenile literature. 3. Chicago White Sox (Baseball team)—Juvenile literature. 4. Batting (Baseball)—Juvenile literature. [1. Thomas, Frank, 1968- . 2. Baseball players. 3. Afro-Americans—Biography.] I. Title. II. Series.
GV865.T45G88   1996
796.357′092—dc20   [B]   95-8831   CIP   AC

Published by The Millbrook Press, Inc.
2 Old New Milford Road
Brookfield, Connecticut 06804

FRANK THOMAS

It was the middle of the 1993 season. The Chicago White Sox were battling for the American League Western Division lead. Each game was important. The White Sox were playing host to the tough New York Yankees at Comiskey Park. It was a close game that was still tied after nine innings.

The New Yorkers failed to score in the top of the 10th. In the bottom of the inning the Yanks had Steve Farr on the mound. Farr was a veteran right-hander who had been the team's bullpen closer the previous few years. He had a fine curveball and sinker. Batters usually hit a lot of ground balls against him.

Stepping to the plate for the White Sox was their 25-year-old first baseman, Frank Thomas. Thomas presented a menacing figure at the plate.

Frank Thomas went on a real batting tear midway through the 1993 season. By this time he was the most feared hitter in the American League. His huge home runs were already legendary.

He stood 6-feet, 5-inches (196 centimeters) tall and weighed nearly 260 pounds (118 kilograms). In the eyes of many, he looked more like a professional football player than a baseball player.

Batting from the right side of the plate, Frank Thomas got set. It was a sight that pitchers were beginning to fear. He was a young hitter with no apparent weakness. And unlike a lot of young power hitters, he didn't flail the bat at bad pitches. In fact, he was one of the most selective hitters in the American League.

But pitcher Steve Farr took up the challenge. After working the count for several pitches, Thomas got one he liked and unleashed his powerful swing. The crack of the bat against the ball was unmistakable. The player known as "The Big Hurt" had hit it hard. Very hard.

The ball rocketed over Farr's head toward center field. At first it looked like a line drive that would be caught by Yankee center fielder Bernie Williams. But the ball kept rising and was still rising as it went over the retreating Williams's head. And it was still rising as it passed over the center field fence for a game-winning home run.

As Frank Thomas trotted around the bases, nearly everyone in the ballpark was still looking out toward center field. Many couldn't believe what they had just seen. Even his teammates and coaches were amazed at how hard the young first sacker had hit the ball. Veteran batting coach Walt Hriniak, who had taught and seen many of the game's great hitters, also found Thomas's hit hard to believe.

"If it hadn't hit the seats, it might still be going," Hriniak said, after the game.

But Frank Thomas had made believers out of nearly everyone since coming up to the White Sox for the first time in August 1990. By the time he whacked his game-winning homer off Steve Farr, he was already considered one of the finest young hitters in the country. And people were beginning to say he was on track to becoming one of the best ever.

A CHILDHOOD TRAGEDY

Frank Edward Thomas was born on May 27, 1968, in Columbus, Georgia. He was the fifth child born to Frank and Charlie Mae Thomas. Both of them worked hard to support their growing family: his father at a bail-bond office, and his mother at a textile mill. While his parents were working, Frank spent a great deal of time with his older brothers and sisters. The Thomas children always looked out for and took care of each other.

Before long, young Frank was following around his older brother Mike, who was already into sports. He tried to keep up with Mike and his friends, but that wasn't always easy.

"I got pushed around a lot until I started pushing back," Frank said, looking back. "So I guess you could say a lot of little hurts went into making 'The Big Hurt.'"

But the hurts weren't always from being knocked around on a football or baseball field. When Frank was seven years old his parents had yet another child, a girl named Pamela. Soon after the baby was born, Charlie Mae Thomas went back to working at the mill . Once again it was up to the older kids to help care for the little one. Because he was the next youngest, Frank always felt very close to little Pamela.

Then one day in September 1977, when Pamela was two-and-a-half, she told her brother she couldn't walk. When she tried, she fell down. The parents quickly took their daughter for tests. The results were devastating to the whole family. Little Pamela had leukemia, a form of cancer. She was admitted to Egleston Children's Hospital in Atlanta for treatment.

Pamela came home once. She had lost her hair from the treatment but still had a big smile on her face. During a relapse she returned to the hospital. On Thanksgiving Day, 1977, she died. That was a day that changed Frank Thomas's life.

"You never get over something like that," he said in 1994. "Right now, she'd be 18 or 19, and it's just not something you can deal with until you've been there."

Some feel that it was his sister Pamela's death that motivated young Frank to become a great baseball player. His father remembered him saying shortly after Pamela died, "Maybe one day I'll be able to do something about it [leukemia]."

When Frank was 13, he was already into sports, playing baseball, basketball, and football. He loved all three. His older brother Mike was starting to get away from sports a bit. One day, their father told Mike to practice his football more and to start lifting weights. Frank, Jr., spoke up and gave his father both advice and a promise: "Daddy, don't fuss with Mike," Frank said. "Mike's gonna be a hard-working man. I'm gonna be the athlete."

A STAR IN THE MAKING

By the time Frank entered Columbus High School, his talent was beginning to develop. He was not a natural athlete who could excel without practice. Then, as now, he had to work very hard.

In fact, when Frank went out for the baseball team for the first time as a freshman, he was cut. So he worked harder. In 1984 he was a member of the state championship team, but he was far from being a star. Then, in 1985, at the end of his junior year, he began to stand out, not only in baseball but in football and basketball as well.

Before long, Frank knew he would have to begin concentrating on just one or two sports in high school. Basketball was the first to go.

"I knew that I wanted to be a professional athlete, but I just didn't know what it would be," he said. "When I got to high school, it became more clear it would be baseball or football."

Columbus High School was a typical suburban school, but Frank was far from being a typical high school athlete. He excelled in baseball, football, and basketball.

A pensive Frank Thomas poses with his many sports trophies at his Columbus, Georgia, home in March 1986. As a senior in high school, Frank was trying to decide whether to play baseball or accept a football scholarship to Auburn University.

As a junior, he starred for the Columbus High gridders, then began putting up some big numbers with the baseball team. He batted .350 that year, with nine home runs. The superior batting eye and power were beginning to show. When he returned for his senior year, there was the same question that plagued many outstanding high school athletes: Which sport would it be?

A big pass receiver, Frank had another fine football season in the fall of 1985. Immediately, the college recruiters began coming around. It began to look as if he was a sure shot for a football scholarship. Then came the 1986 baseball season.

This time Frank really began tearing up the diamond. Playing for Coach Bobby Howard, he was without a doubt one of the most powerful and dangerous hitters in the state. Already close to his full height and weighing well over 200 pounds (91 kilograms), he hit with tremendous power. But he also hit for average and had a keen batting eye. Even in high school he wasn't just a wild swinger.

The Columbus team would finish with a 25–5 record that year. And the team leader was undoubtedly big Frank Thomas. He finished the year with a .450 batting average, 13 home runs and 52 runs batted in. Those were outstanding numbers for a 30-game season. After it ended, he was named an All-State performer and also Bi-City Player-of-the-Year. Now it was time for the big decision.

Frank was offered a full football scholarship to Auburn University in Alabama. Auburn wanted him to be a tight end. With his size, speed, and athletic ability, he looked like a potential All-American. Several other schools also wanted him as a football player. But Auburn was the only one that said he could play baseball as well.

There was something else to consider, however. It was time for the annual major-league baseball amateur draft. Frank was eager for a pro career. He decided that if he was drafted, he would not go to Auburn. Instead, he would sign with any major league team that picked him.

Frank and his father waited for three days until the draft was over. In all, 1,423 amateur players were chosen. But despite his size, superior numbers, and powerful bat, he wasn't picked by any one of the big-league clubs. It seems that many of the baseball scouts believed he was all set to go to Auburn and didn't want to chance wasting a draft pick.

When he learned he wasn't drafted, Frank went up to his room and cried. As one writer put it, he would have signed "for a plane ticket and a pack of chewing gum." But at least he had another way to go. In the fall of 1986 he left Columbus for Auburn University, where he had accepted the football scholarship.

FRESHMAN ALL-AMERICAN

Under Coach Pat Dye, the Auburn Tigers had a topflight Division I football program. With Bo Jackson running the football, the Tigers had often been in the national spotlight over the past three years. Frank was really looking forward to playing with the team. As a freshman, however, he had to play behind starting tight end Walter Reevers and the more experienced Lee Mark Sellers. So he didn't see much action.

As a part-time player, Frank caught just three passes for 45 yards during the entire season. But Frank hated sitting on the bench, and that spring he decided to try another plan. Instead of going back to spring football practice, he walked onto the baseball diamond and told coach Hal Baird that he wanted to try out for the team.

There were many scholarship players in the Tigers' ballclub, and walk-ons rarely have a chance to start. But after just the first day of practice, Coach Baird knew that Frank Thomas wasn't just another walk-on.

"He was one of those rare athletes that, the very first time we saw him on our field, we realized he was something special," the coach said.

By the time the season opened, Frank was starting first baseman. And within just a few games, it was apparent to everyone that he was by far the best hitter on the team. In fact, he was a monster.

The second game of the 1987 season was against the University of Alabama at Birmingham. Frank got four hits in five times at bat. Better yet, he whacked a grand slam home run and also had a three-run blast as the Tigers won, 23-2. He was on his way and didn't falter all year.

When the season ended, Frank Thomas was considered one of the best freshman players in the country. That was confirmed when he was named to the freshman All-America team. In 59 games he had 75 hits in 209 at bats for an impressive .359 average. Among those hits were 12 doubles and a school record 21 home runs. He also drove in 68 runs, more than an RBI a game, and had a slugging percentage of .718.

Frank was a third-string tight end as an Auburn freshman in 1987. But he was still considered a fine prospect until a knee injury the following year led him to concentrate on baseball.

His coach called him the greatest walk-on baseball player in Southeastern Conference (SEC) history. That summer, he became one of 30 players chosen as a member of the U.S. National Team. The team would play 27 games over the summer. Then, 20 members of the team would be chosen to represent the United States at the Pan Am Games in late summer.

The tour took the U.S. National team around the United States and also to Cuba. Frank was the youngest member. He started most of the games as the designated hitter and soon found out he could hit the ball as well as or better than anyone.

"Nobody on the team had the power I had," he said.

But while he was playing extremely well, Frank knew he had to make a decision about football. If he stayed with the team and was chosen for the Pan Am Games, he would miss Auburn's early fall football practice. Finally, he told Coach Ron Fraser that he was leaving the team to return to Auburn.

"He was pretty surprised at first," Frank said. "Some of the other players didn't understand it either. Coach Baird at Auburn knew I wanted to play on the Olympic team in 1988, and he thought my leaving would hurt my chances. But Coach Fraser said he would still recommend me for the [Olympic] team."

So Frank returned to Auburn with the idea of becoming the starting tight end for the football team.

AN EYE ON THE MAJORS

Frank was very serious about football in the fall of 1987, but sometimes things don't work out the way you want. He looked good in the early conditioning drills. Then, on just the third day, with the team wearing pads for contact, it happened. Freshman running back Shayne Wasden collided with Frank on a broken play. Wasden got up, but Frank didn't. He was down and holding his knee.

The diagnosis was strained ligaments. Frank was expected to be out four to six weeks. It turned out to be more than that: The injury kept him out all year; in fact, he never played football again.

Being injured gave Frank time to think about his priorities. He knew he had had very limited success in football, having played infrequently as a freshman and then losing his sophomore year to injury. In baseball, however, he was already a freshman All-American and had excelled on the U.S. National Team. He decided to look at his knee injury as a chance for a successful career in baseball.

"I really knew by that point that I could be a professional baseball player," he said.

So from then on, Frank Thomas concentrated solely on becoming the best baseball player he could be. When he reported for baseball practice in the spring of 1988, he was ready to go. Frank had another outstanding season. He homered in his first at bat and went on from there. He had two homers in a 10–3 win over Vanderbilt and was 4 for 5 with a two-run homer, an RBI double, and five runs batted in against Tennessee. His best game came against Jacksonville State when he also went 4 for 5, cracking a pair of three-run homers and driving in eight runs.

When the season ended, Frank was the leading hitter in the SEC with a .385 average in 55 games. He led the team in eight offensive categories and was a First Team All-SEC choice for the second straight year. Only his power numbers were down. He finished with nine home runs and 54 RBIs. SEC pitchers were working him more carefully, not giving him as many good pitches to hit. And Frank Thomas simply didn't swing at bad pitches.

His biggest letdown came after the season when he wasn't chosen for the U.S. Olympic baseball team. But, as usual, Frank turned a negative into a positive. He was a man who hated failure, so he continued to work even harder to build his body and improve his skills.

"I decided during the off-season to work harder on all phases of my

game," he said. "I studied films, took more cuts in the batting cage, and concentrated on my defensive play."

When he returned for the 1989 season, he quickly showed he was one of the most powerful and skilled collegiate hitters in the country. From the very first game he was ripping the hide off the ball while showing much-improved play in the field. Now the big-league scouts were watching him all the time. His ability as a hitter was obvious to everyone.

With the season already past the halfway mark, Coach Baird couldn't say enough. "At this point in time I'd say he's the best hitter I've ever coached," Baird told the press. "People just stop what they're doing to watch Frank take batting practice.

"Frank has done all he can do at this level," the coach continued. "He's seen all the good pitchers in the league and hammered them consistently. It's time for him to see 90-mile-per-hour fastballs every day. He's done nothing this spring to diminish his stock."

With the major-league draft about a month away in June, Frank knew what he wanted. He was still in a hurry to prove his worth, and once he signed with a big-league team, he was anxious to prove himself against the best.

"I don't want to hang around in the minor leagues," he said. "College ball is close to single A, and I know I can play at this level. I'd like to start out at double A, but I want to go to the show [the majors] quickly. If they think I need to stay down for a while, then I'll just work hard and prove them wrong."

This soon became a familiar sight at Auburn: Frank gets a high-five from a teammate as he crosses the plate after still another home run. His coach, Hal Baird, said he knew Frank was something special the very first time he saw him play.

When the Auburn season ended, Frank had become a bona fide All-American. He led the SEC in hitting with an impressive .403 average in 64 games. He was second in homers with 19, led the conference in RBIs with 83, and had an amazing slugging percentage of .801. His 49 career homers were an Auburn record, and his 73 bases on balls in 1989 were yet another school mark.

Then he waited for the draft. He was the seventh player taken in the first round, picked by the Chicago White Sox.

It was finally time to leave Auburn. Looking back, Frank knew he would have signed out of high school if someone had drafted him then. But he had no regrets about spending three years at college.

"Sure I would have signed then," he said. "But nobody wanted me. As it turned out, going to Auburn made me a man."

BECOMING THE BIG HURT

Maybe the toughest thing about being a first-year pro is the length of the season. College players like Frank are used to a 55-60 game collegiate season. But once a collegian signs, he has to continue playing beyond the already completed college season. As soon as he signed with the White Sox, Frank was sent to Sarasota, Florida, in the Gulf Coast League, which is a rookie league.

An All-American at Auburn in 1989, Frank looked comfortable, yet imposing, in his baseball uniform. His smile got even bigger when he learned that the Chicago White Sox had made him the seventh player taken in the first round of the 1989 amateur draft.

There he played just 16 games, immediately hitting well. He had 16 hits in 48 at bats for a .333 average, including five doubles, one homer and 11 RBIs. The White Sox had seen enough. They promoted him to their Sarasota team in the Florida State League. This was class A ball.

Frank played an additional 55 games at Sarasota in 1989, for a total of 135 games, more than twice what he was used to playing. That might have accounted for the .277 average he had at class A Sarasota. In addition, he had four homers and 30 RBIs in 188 times at bat. It was the only time, thus far, that he had hit under .300.

His goal, however, was to make the White Sox in 1990. During spring training he ripped the baseball as well as anyone in camp. He batted over .500 and slammed a pair of home runs, one of them off the great Nolan Ryan. It looked as if he had made the club, if not as a first baseman then as a designated hitter. But just before the final cuts, the Sox shocked everyone by sending Frank to the double A Birmingham Barons of the Southern League.

The reason, the Sox said, was his defense. "We drafted him to be a first baseman and an everyday player," said general manager Larry Hines, "not just a designated hitter."

Once again, Frank was bitterly disappointed. His father said it was the third time Frank had been devastated. "First was the day we lost my baby girl," Frank, Sr., said, "Then the day no one drafted him out of high school and now the day he was sent back to the minors."

But Frank had always overcome disappointment with determination and hard work. In Birmingham he hit the baseball better than anyone in the league. He was doing it all. His batting average stayed above .300. As usual, he had a sharp eye and was leading the league in walks. But he was also among the leaders in homers and RBIs. It was apparent he wouldn't be in the minors for long.

"He has excellent discipline at the plate," said his manager, Ken Berry, himself a former big-league outfielder. "He can hit the ball to all fields and hit off-speed [pitches] as well as the fast ball."

By August, the White Sox knew they could wait no longer. In 109 games with Birmingham, Frank was hitting .323 with 18 homers and 71 RBIs. He also had 27 doubles, 5 triples, and walked 112 times. On August 2, Frank Thomas got his ticket to the majors. And while he didn't finish the Birmingham season, he would later be named Minor League Player of the Year by *Baseball America*.

Now Frank vowed to stay in the majors. To do that, his bat would have to do the talking. The Sox also wanted to see what he could do, so they put him in the lineup immediately.

In 60 games, Frank's average in the majors was even better than it had been in the minors. He whacked away at a .330 clip. As usual, he was consistent. He had hits in 45 of the 60 games, including one streak of 13 straight. On September 24, during that hitting streak, Frank was named American League Player of the Week.

He had 11 doubles, 3 triples, 7 homers, and 31 RBIs. He even played well at first with a .989 fielding percentage. In addition, he had a .529 slugging average. There was no doubt he had proved his worth to the White Sox. His .330 batting average was the highest by a Sox player with at least 200 plate appearances since 1942. Best yet, he had achieved another of his goals: His trip through the minors had been a very short one. He was with the White Sox to stay.

In 1991, Frank was a big part of the White Sox's plans. Chicago had a solid club. Robin Ventura, Dan Pasqua, and Carlton Fisk provided power; Tim Raines, Ozzie Guillen, and Lance Johnson had excellent speed. Right-hander Jack McDowell was an emerging star, and the young righties Alex Fernandez and Melido Perez looked promising. Veterans Charley Hough, Greg Hibbard, Bobby Thigpen, and Scott Radinsky gave the club good, though not great, pitching.

What the team lacked was a real superstar, a big man who could carry them for several stretches during the year. It was hoped that Frank would be that man. He wound up being a designated hitter nearly twice as often as playing first, but his hitting was consistently good no matter where he played.

Once again Frank was a .300-plus hitter with power. He became the most feared hitter on the team almost immediately, and one of the most feared in the league. Not only did he have the best batting average on the team, but he was their leader in homers and RBIs as well. And he still had a fine batting eye. While doing all the heavy hitting, he was also on course to break the team record for walks. Being patient was part of his batting style.

"I take a lot of pitches," Frank explained. "I'd like to see everything the pitcher has in the first at bat if I can. And if I'm going to make an out, I'm going to make an out on a pitch I can hit."

It was a real battle in the American League West in 1991. The Sox, Twins, Rangers, Royals, and Mariners were all close to the top and often bunched

Frank hit his way through the minor leagues and came up with the White Sox in August 1990. He said he was determined to stay and let his bat do the talking. He started hitting and never stopped. Here he smacks another base hit early in the 1991 season.

together. By August 11, the Twins had a 67–45 record, with the White Sox just a single game behind. Unfortunately, the team faded down the stretch and wound up with an 87–75 mark for the year, finishing second in the division, eight games behind the Twins.

But for Frank, it had been an outstanding first full year, with achieving a .318 batting average, clubbing 32 home runs, and driving in 109 runs. He also scored 104 times. He was ninth in the league in hitting, fifth in both homers and RBIs. He led the league with 138 walks and also topped the American League with an on-base percentage of .453, an incredible mark for a young slugger.

Better yet, he finished third (behind Cal Ripken and Cecil Fielder) in the Most Valuable Player voting. He was also named

By the end of 1991, Frank was already one of the best hitters in baseball. But he worked on his fielding, too. Here he tags the Angels' Luis Polonia on an attempted pickoff play. Polonia just made it back in time.

to both the Associated Press and *Sporting News* All-Star teams. He had proved to everyone that he could flat-out play.

And it was also during the 1991 season that he got his nickname. It was given to him by the colorful White Sox announcer, former player Ken "Hawk" Harrelson. Watching the way Frank could hammer the baseball, Harrelson was the first to call him "The Big Hurt."

AN ALL-STAR AND
MOST VALUABLE PLAYER

As successful as the 1991 season had been, Frank Thomas knew that one great year didn't make a career.

"It's fine what you're doing for the moment," he said, "but when you start doing something six, seven, eight years in a row, then you can start making comparisons. I'm working as hard as ever."

During the spring of 1992 he noticed that American League pitchers were working to him more carefully. "I've shown I can hit the long ball and they're going to try to keep me from doing it," he said.

Again he showed maturity far beyond his years. He would take what they gave him. If he couldn't hit a home run, he would settle for a single or double. . . or a walk. The White Sox were hoping for the divisional title. But injuries and inconsistent pitching left them in third place at 86–76, 10 games behind Oakland.

Frank Thomas proved once again, however, that he was one of the finest young hitters in all of baseball. This time The Big Hurt clubbed away at a .323 pace, the third-highest average in the American League. Because the

*"The Big Hurt" in 1992. He looks like he's enjoying
every minute as a big-league superstar.*

pitchers were being more careful, his home run total dropped to 24. But he
drove home 115 runs, also third best in the league. That wasn't all. Frank tied
for first in walks with 122 and in doubles with 46. He led the league with 72
extra-base hits and also with a .439 on-base percentage. He was second in
runs scored with 108, fourth in total bases with 307, and fifth in hits with
185. It was a superb season for a 24-year-old.

More and more people began to marvel at his amazing skills with the bat. Cleveland hurler Dennis Martinez spoke for many pitchers when he said that "pitchers shouldn't be left out there alone with him."

Frank had always been a very confident player. Yet he continued to work hard to improve. His father felt it was his belief in himself that made him even better.

"Frank believes he's a great hitter," said Mr. Thomas. "There's absolutely no doubt in his mind. I think that kind of makes him go, makes him even better, day to day."

In 1993 the Sox felt they were ready to make a run at the divisional title. McDowell and Fernandez were joined by Wilson Alvarez and Jason Bere to form a big four on the mound. Frank would have help in the power department from Ventura, Raines, newcomer Ellis Burks, emerging catcher Ron Karkovice, and Bo

Frank was off to another big start in 1993. On April 30, he belted a grand slam home run against the Toronto Blue Jays. Here his happy teammates greet him after he circled the bases.

Jackson. With speedsters Lance Johnson, Ozzie Guillen, and Joey Cora the Sox seemed like the best in the West.

And the Sox were the best, steaming to a divisional title with a 94–68 record. McDowell won 22 games, Fernandez 18, Alvarez 15, and Bere 12. The club had the best pitching in the league. Almost all the hitters had fine seasons, giving the team a balance of power and average, but the biggest man of all was again Frank Thomas.

The Big Hurt put together a truly remarkable season. He had a .317 batting average, smacked a career best 41 homers, and had a personal best of 128 runs batted in. He was in the top ten in nine offensive categories, set a franchise home run record, and was American League Player of the Month in August when the Sox drove toward the divisional crown.

In addition, Frank became just the fifth player in baseball history to bat over .300 with 20 home runs, 100 RBIs, 100 runs scored, and 100 walks in three consecutive seasons. The others who did it were Babe Ruth, Lou Gehrig, Jimmie Foxx, and Ted Williams. They were all-time greats, enshrined in the Hall of Fame. Frank had done it by the time he was 25 years old. He also made the American League All-Star team for the first time.

But even with all his hitting feats, the thing he was most proud of was his improvement in the field.

"My favorite moment this year was a play I made at first," Frank said. "I dove to my right, then threw home to get the runner. I don't think I could have made that play before this year."

He still wanted to be recognized as a great all-around player. Being just a superior hitter wasn't enough.

Frank has always worked hard to improve his fielding. Here he is in action on a pickoff attempt against the A's Ricky Henderson.

But there was a problem toward the end of the 1993 season. On September 19, a week after he hit his 41st home run, Frank tried to make a catch of a foul near the stands and banged his left arm into the fence. He suffered a deep bruise to his triceps muscle. He played a few games with the injury, then didn't play from September 27 to the end of the season, missing the final nine games.

Now the Sox had to meet the defending world champion Toronto Blue Jays in the American League Championship Series. The winner of the best-of-seven battle would go to the World Series. Frank said right away that he would try to play.

As it turned out, the Blue Jays had too much firepower for the White Sox. They won in six games. Frank played in all six, but got just 17 at bats. He still hit .353, but the injury to his arm cut down on his power. His only extra-base hit was a home run, and he drove in just three. Many felt a healthy Frank Thomas could have made the difference.

After the season, Frank received the ultimate honor. He was named the American League's Most Valuable Player. Not only that, it was a unanimous selection. He was named on every single ballot, only the 10th player in baseball history to be chosen in that way.

At age 25, there was no telling how far The Big Hurt could go.

THE SKY'S THE LIMIT

The 1994 season opened under a dark cloud. The players' union didn't have a new contract with the owners. They said from the outset that if an agreement wasn't reached soon, there might be a players' strike sometime late in the sea-

A relaxed Frank Thomas speaks to the media in Chicago after learning he had been selected the American League's Most Valuable Player for 1993. He was only the tenth player in baseball history to be a unanimous selection.

son. But guys like Frank Thomas and the other stars couldn't think about that. They had to concentrate on baseball and helping their teams to win.

Under Manager Gene Lamont, the White Sox wanted another crack at getting to the World Series. Early on it appeared to be the year of the hitter, players in both leagues whacking home runs and hitting for high averages. And Frank Thomas, in just his fourth full season, looked better than ever.

Before the season began, he had signed a multiyear contract extension worth more than $40 million. He was now signed through 1998, with options for 1999 and the year 2000. But Frank didn't allow himself to get caught up in his own celebrity. Over his locker were the letters "D.B.T.H." That stood for *Don't Believe the Hype.*

Frank explained: "If you start reading that stuff and get caught up in it, you will slip. I'm not concerned about being the big man in town. I just want to continue to improve. I believe I can do some things that have never been done before. I want to be a great ballplayer. I want to be a Hall of Famer."

The Yankees' Paul O'Neill had his average up over .400 for a good part of the first half of the season. Meanwhile, Frank, Cleveland's Albert Belle, and Seattle's Ken Griffey, Jr., were having incredible, all-around power-plus-average seasons. In the eyes of many, Frank had the best total offensive skills.

By mid-season, the White Sox were again battling for the American League Central Division, while Frank was hitting around .350 and was up among the leaders in all batting categories. He was named a starter on the All-Star team. He had two hits in the game and smacked the two longest homers in the home run hitting contest, one traveling 519 feet (158 meters).

"Frank is doing things I've never seen in seventeen years in the major leagues," said Toronto's Paul Molitor, a future Hall of Famer himself.

Teammate Julio Franco put it this way. "Playing with Frank is like being part of history."

And Ken Harrelson, who watched Thomas day after day from the broadcasting booth, couldn't believe how Frank continued to improve. Harrelson felt the sky was the limit.

Even in the dugout Frank stays in the game. You can almost feel his intensity as he waits to get back in action early in 1994.

"Thirty years from now, if you take a poll of 100 hitters, they'll say that Frank Thomas is the best hitter who ever lived." That might have been jumping the gun a bit, the kind of hype Frank tried to ignore. But he was American League Player of the Month in May and again in July. He seemed to be getting stronger. There was talk of him winning the triple crown (batting average, homers, and RBIs), and maybe breaking Babe Ruth's long-standing record for runs scored. Some thought that Frank even had a chance to break Roger Maris's single season record of 61 home runs.

But it all ended on August 12. That's when the players made good their threat to go on strike. When the two sides could not reach an agreement for a new contract, the remainder of the season and the World Series were canceled. It was the first time since 1904 that the World Series wouldn't be played. At the time of the strike the White Sox had a record of 67–46, leading the American League Central Division by one game over Cleveland. It would have been an exciting race to the finish.

No American League catcher wants to face the prospect of the 250-pound (113-kilogram) Big Hurt bearing down on him. Here Frank slides under Toronto catcher Pat Borders, and scores all the way from first on a double.

It also would have been a great finish for Frank. In 113 games he had had a season that most players never have in a full 162. He was third behind O'Neill and Belle in hitting at .353. He finished second to Griffey in homers with 38 and tied for third with 101 RBIs. He led the league in slugging (.729), in on-base percentage (.487), in walks (109), and runs scored (106). His slugging percentage was the highest since Ted Williams had a .731 mark in 1957.

The 1994 season ended abruptly on August 12, when the Players' Association called a strike against the owners. Although he hated not playing, Frank stayed out with his teammates. At left, he leaves Comiskey Park with some personal items. Despite the early end of the 1994 season, Frank was named the American League's Most Valuable Player for the second straight year. Here he accepts congratulations from the press, with his wife Elise and daughter Sloane at his side.

Even in the short season, he became the third player in history (with Lou Gehrig and Ted Williams) to bat .300 with 20 or more homers, 100 or more RBIs, 100 or more walks, and 100 or more runs scored four seasons in a row.

Despite the short season and no playoffs, individual awards were still given. To the surprise of no one, Frank Thomas was again named the American League's Most Valuable Player. He was only the 11th player in history to win that honor two years in a row.

During his time in the major leagues, Frank Thomas has made a name for himself as more than just a great ballplayer. While many players today charge $10 or $20, or even more, to sign an autograph, Frank Thomas charges just one dollar. And he does that for a special reason: For every autograph he signs, he matches the dollar and sends the proceeds to the Leukemia Society of America in memory of his sister Pamela. The money from the sale of his special Gold Leaf baseball cards also goes to the Leukemia Society.

In 1993, Frank established the Frank Thomas Charitable Foundation, which assists children and others in need. He also participates in the United Way Crusade of Mercy Home Run High Program. When people think of Frank Thomas, they think of a superstar who is giving back.

In 1991, Frank married Elise Silver. Their son, Sterling Edward, was born in 1992, and their daughter, Sloane, arrived two years later. Although Frank and his wife come from different backgrounds and different parts of

Although he would rather be using his bat to hit big-league pitching, Frank grabbed the lumber to pose for a clothing store advertisement in Chicago during the players' strike of 1994.

the country (she's from Rochester, New York), Elise Thomas has an explanation for why their relationship works so well. "When you come from two loving families, it's pretty easy," she has said.

Some have said that the strike of 1994 took away one of the greatest seasons a hitter ever had. No one knows what Frank would have done if the schedule had been completed. But he still has a long way to go. At the end of 1994 he was just 26 years old with already four years in the majors.

It's clear that Frank Thomas can only get better because he has always worked hard and will continue to do so. As he has said himself, "I followed my dreams and I worked hard to get where I am today. Nothing's easy for me. I did this all myself."

When baseball resumed in 1995, Frank Thomas showed he hadn't missed a beat. Once again he was up among the American League leaders in all offensive categories. And his long home runs were still the talk of the league.

FRANK THOMAS: HIGHLIGHTS

1968   Born on May 27 in Columbus, Georgia.

1984   Columbus High School wins Georgia state baseball championship.

1986   Named All-State high school baseball player.
Enters Auburn University in Alabama on a football scholarship.

1987   Joins Auburn baseball team as a walk-on player.
Named to college freshman All-America baseball team.
Chosen as a member of the U.S. National Baseball Team.

1988   Leads Southeastern Conference (SEC) in hitting.
Named to All-SEC first team.

1989   Leads SEC in hitting; named All-American.
Drafted by Chicago White Sox; plays 16 games for Sox's rookie team, Sarasota
(Florida) of the Gulf Coast League; promoted to Sox's Class A team, Sarasota of the
Florida State League.

1990   Promoted to Sox's Double-A team, Birmingham Barons of the Southern League.
Named Minor League Player of the Year.
Promoted to White Sox in August; bats .330 in 60 major-league games.

1991   In first full season in majors, hits .318 with 32 home runs and 109 RBIs.
Leads American League with 138 walks and .453 on-base percentage.
Marries Elise Silver.

1992   Hits .323 with 24 home runs and 115 RBIs.
Leads league in extra-base hits (72) and on-base percentage (.439). Ties for league lead
in walks (122) and doubles (46).

1993   Named American League's Most Valuable Player.
Hits .317 with 41 home runs and 128 RBIs.
Named to American League All-Star team.
Establishes Frank Thomas Charitable Foundation.

1994   Named American League's Most Valuable Player.
In 113 games (strike-shortened season), hits .353 with 38 home runs and 101 RBIs.
Signs multiyear contract.

1995   Had another great season, with a .308 batting average, 40 home runs, and 111 RBIs.

FIND OUT MORE

Cox, Ted. *Frank Thomas: The Big Hurt*. Chicago: Childrens Press, 1994.

Feldman, Jay. *Hitting*. New York: Simon and Schuster, 1991.

Gutman, Bill. *Baseball*. North Bellmore, N.Y.: Marshall Cavendish, 1990.

Kaplan, Rick. *The Official Baseball Hall of Fame Book of Super Stars*. New York: Simon and Schuster, 1989.

Monteleone, John. *A Day in the Life of a Major League Baseball Player*. Mahwah, N.J.: Troll, 1992.

How to write to Frank Thomas:

Frank Thomas
c/o Chicago White Sox
333 West 35th Street
Chicago, IL
60616

INDEX